With Christmas wishes

To _____

From _____

Michael Hague's
Family
Christmas Treasury

Henry Holt and Company
New York

Permission for the use of the following is gratefully acknowledged:

Page 18: "Carol of the Brown King" by Langston Hughes. Copyright © 1958 by Crisis Publishing Company. Copyright renewed 1986 by George Houston Bass. Reprinted by permission of Harold Ober Associates Incorporated.

Page 80: "In the Week When Christmas Comes" from Eleanor Farjeon's *Poems for Children* by Eleanor Farjeon. "In the Week When Christmas Comes" originally appeared in *Come Christmas* by Eleanor Farjeon. Copyright © 1927, 1955 by Eleanor Farjeon. Selection reprinted by permission of HarperCollins Publishers.

Page 84: "little tree" is reprinted from *Complete Poems, 1904–1962*, by E. E. Cummings, edited by George L. Firmage, by permission of Liveright Publishing Corporation. Copyright © 1925, 1953, 1991 by the Trustees for the E. E. Cummings Trust. Copyright © 1976 by George James Firmage.

Page 89: Excerpt from Dylan Thomas: *A Child's Christmas in Wales.* Copyright © 1952 by Dylan Thomas. Reprinted by permission of New Directions Publishing Corporation.

Page 93: Excerpt from *A Christmas Memory* by Truman Capote. Copyright © 1956 by Truman Capote. Reprinted by permission of Random House, Inc.

Henry Holt and Company, Inc. / *Publishers since 1866*
115 West 18th Street / New York, New York 10011

Henry Holt is a registered trademark of Henry Holt and Company, Inc.
Illustrations copyright © 1995 by Michael Hague
Musical arrangements copyright © 1995 by Shaun Naidoo
All rights reserved.
Published in Canada by Fitzhenry & Whiteside Ltd.,
195 Allstate Parkway, Markham, Ontario L3R 4T8.

Library of Congress Cataloging-in-Publication Data
Michael Hague's family Christmas treasury.
p.   cm.
Summary: Stories, poems, and music associated with Christmas.
1. Christmas—Literary collections. [1. Christmas—Literary collections.]
I. Hague, Michael, ill.
PZ5.M58863   1996   95-6068

ISBN 0-8050-1011-4
First Edition—1995
The artist used mixed media on watercolor board
to create the illustrations for this book.
Printed in the United States of America on acid-free paper. ∞

1   3   5   7   9   10   8   6   4   2

Contents

The Story of Christmas

The Spirit of Christmas

The Celebration of Christmas

Michael Hague's

❄ Family ❄
Christmas Treasury

The Story
of Christmas

The Gospel
According to St. Luke
1:27–33

King James Version

The angel Gabriel was sent from God unto a city of Galilee, named Nazareth, to a virgin espoused to a man whose name was Joseph, of the house of David; and the virgin's name was Mary. And the angel came in unto her, and said, Hail, thou that are highly favoured, the Lord is with thee: blessed art thou among women. And when she saw him, she was troubled at his saying, and cast in her mind what manner of salutation this should be. And the angel said unto her, Fear not, Mary: for thou has found favour with God. And, behold, thou shalt conceive in thy womb, and bring forth a son, and shalt call his name JESUS. He shall be great, and shall be called the Son of the Highest: and the Lord God shall give unto him the throne of his father David: And he shall reign over the house of Jacob for ever; and of his kingdom there shall be no end.

Once in Royal David's City

1. Once in roy - al Dav - id's ci - ty, Stood a low - ly cat - tle - shed, Where a
2. He came down to earth from hea - ven, Who is God and Lord of all, And His
3. Not in that poor low - ly sta - ble, With the ox - en stand - ing by, We shall

moth - er laid her ba - by, In a man - ger for His bed; Ma - ry
shel - ter was a sta - ble, And His cra - dle was a stall; With the
see Him; but in hea - ven, Set at God's right hand on high; When like

was that moth - er mild, Je - sus Christ her lit - tle - child.
poor, and mean, and low - ly, Lived on earth our Sav - ior ho - ly.
stars His chil - dren crowned, All in white shall wait a - round.

The Gospel
According to St. Luke
2:1–14

King James Version

And it came to pass in those days, that there went out a decree from Caesar Augustus, that all the world should be taxed. (And this taxing was first made when Cyrenius was governor of Syria.) And all went to be taxed, every one into his own city. And Joseph also went up from Galilee, out of the city of Nazareth, into Judaea, unto the city of David, which is called Bethlehem (because he was of the house and lineage of David): To be taxed with Mary his espoused wife, being great with child. And so it was, that, while they were there, the days were accomplished that she should be delivered. And she brought forth her firstborn son, and wrapped him in swaddling clothes, and laid him in a manger; because there was no room for them in the inn. And there were in the same country shepherds abiding in the field, keeping watch over their flock by night. And, lo, the angel of the Lord came upon them, and the glory of the Lord shone round about them: and they were sore afraid. And the angel said unto them, Fear not: for, behold, I bring you good tidings of great joy, which shall be to all people. For unto you is born this day in the city of David a Saviour, which is Christ the Lord. And this shall be a sign unto you; Ye shall find the babe wrapped in swaddling clothes, lying in a manger. And suddenly there was with the angel a multitude of the heavenly host praising God, and saying, Glory to God in the highest, and on earth peace, good will toward men.

Away in a Manger

Gently

1. A - way in a man - ger, no crib for a bed, The
2. The cat - tle are low - ing, the poor ba - by wakes, But

lit - tle Lord Je - sus laid down His sweet head, The
lit - tle Lord Je - sus, no cry - ing He makes, I

stars in the sky, - looked down where He lay, The
love Thee, Lord Je - sus, look down from the sky, And

lit - tle Lord Je - sus, a - sleep on the hay.
stay by my cra - dle, till morn - ing is nigh.

While Shepherds Watched
Their Flocks by Night

3. "To you in David's town this day,
   Is born of David's line
   The Savior, Who is Christ the Lord;
   And this shall be the sign:

4. "The heav'nly Babe you there shall find,
   To human view displayed,
   All meanly wrapp'd in swathing bands,
   And in a manger laid."

5. Thus spake the seraph, and forthwith
   Appear'd a shining throng
   Of angels praising God, who thus
   Address'd their joyful song:

6. "All glory be to God on high,
   And to the earth be peace;
   Good will henceforth from heav'n to men
   Begin and never cease."

The Gospel
According to St. Matthew
2:1–15

King James Version

Now when Jesus was born in Bethlehem of Judea in the days of Herod the king, behold, there came wise men from the east to Jerusalem, saying, Where is he that is born King of the Jews? for we have seen his star in the east, and are come to worship him. When Herod the king had heard these things, he was troubled, and all Jerusalem with him. And when he had gathered all the chief priests and scribes of the people together, he demanded of them where Christ should be born. And they said unto him, In Bethlehem of Judea: for thus it is written by the prophet, and thou Bethlehem in the land of Juda, art not the least among the princes of Juda: for out of thee shall come a Governor, that shall rule my people Israel. Then Herod, when he had privily called the wise men, inquired of them diligently what time the star appeared. And he sent them to Bethlehem, and said, Go and search diligently for the young child; and when ye have found him, bring me word again, that I may come and worship him also. When they had heard the king, they departed; and lo, the star, which they saw in the east, went before them, till it came and stood over where the young child was. When they saw the star, they rejoiced with exceeding great joy. And when they were come into the house, they saw the young child with Mary his mother, and fell down, and worshipped him: and when they had opened their treasures, they presented unto him gifts; gold, and frankincense, and myrrh. And being warned of God in a dream that they should not return to Herod, they departed into their own country another way. And when they were departed, behold, the angel of the Lord appeareth to Joseph in a dream, saying, Arise, and take the young child and his mother, and flee into Egypt, and be thou there until I bring thee word: for Herod will seek the young child to destroy him. When he arose, he took the young child and his mother by night, and departed into Egypt: And was there until the death of Herod: that it might be fulfilled which was spoken of the Lord by the prophet, saying, Out of Egypt have I called my son.

We Three Kings of Orient Are

1. We three kings of O-ri-ent are, Bear-ing gifts we tra-verse a-far,
2. Born a babe on Beth-le-hem's plain, Gold we bring to crown Him a-gain;

Field and foun-tain, moor and moun-tain, Fol-low-ing yon-der Star.
King for-ev-er, ceas-ing nev-er, O-ver us all to reign.

Refrain

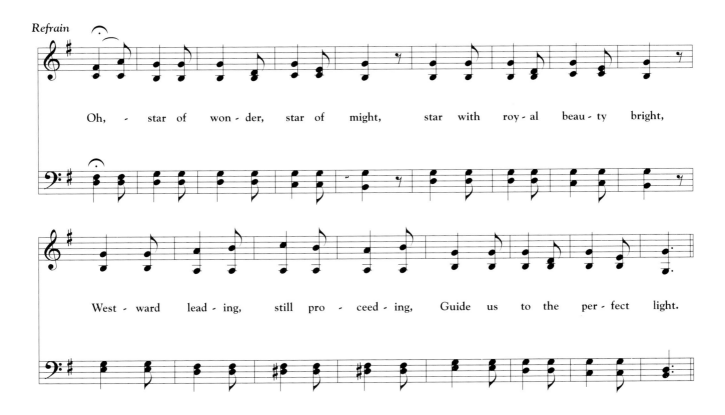

Oh, - star of won - der, star of might, star with roy - al beau - ty bright,

West - ward lead - ing, still pro - ceed - ing, Guide us to the per - fect light.

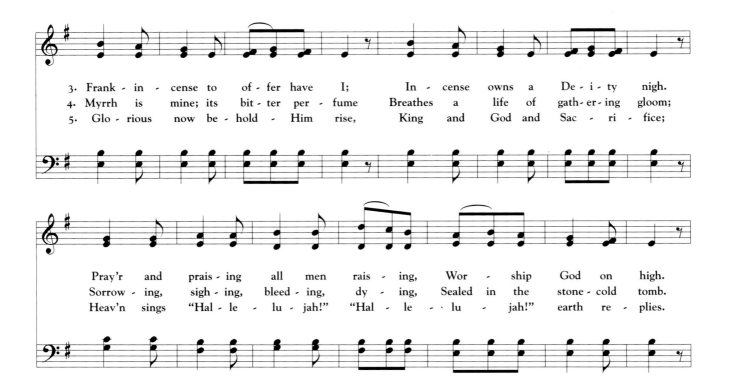

3. Frank - in - cense to of - fer have I; In - cense owns a De - i - ty nigh.
4. Myrrh is mine; its bit - ter per - fume Breathes a life of gath - er - ing gloom;
5. Glo - rious now be - hold - Him rise, King and God and Sac - ri - fice;

Pray'r and prais - ing all men rais - ing, Wor - ship God on high.
Sorrow - ing, sigh - ing, bleed - ing, dy - ing, Sealed in the stone - cold tomb.
Heav'n sings "Hal - le - lu - jah!" "Hal - le - lu - jah!" earth re - plies.

Refrain

Oh, - star of won - der, star of might, star with roy - al beau - ty bright,

West - ward lead - ing, still pro - ceed - ing, Guide us to the per - fect light.

Carol of the Brown King

Langston Hughes

Of the three Wise Men
Who came to the King,
One was a brown man,
So they sing.

Of the three Wise Men
Who followed the Star,
One was a brown king
From afar.

They brought fine gifts
Of spices and gold
In jewelled boxes
Of beauty untold.

Unto His humble
Manger they came
And bowed their heads
In Jesus' name.

Three Wise Men,
One dark like me—
Part of His
Nativity.

The Spirit
of Christmas

Silent Night

Peacefully

1. Si - lent night! Ho - ly night! All is calm, all is bright.
2. Si - lent night! Ho - ly night! Shep - herds quake at the sight!
3. Si - lent night! Ho - ly night! Son of God, love's pure light!

'Round yon vir - gin moth - er and child! Ho - ly In - fant, so ten - der and mild,
Glo - ries stream - from heav - en a - far, Heav'n - ly hosts - sing, "Al - le - lu - ia!"
Ra - diant beams - from Thy ho - ly face, With the dawn of re - deem - ing grace,

Sleep in heav - en - ly peace, Sleep - in heav - en - ly peace.
Christ, the Sav - ior, is born! Christ, - the Sav - ior, is born!
Je - sus, Lord at Thy birth, Je - sus, Lord at Thy birth.

O Come, All Ye Faithful

Adeste Fideles

Fervently

1. O come all ye faith - ful, Joy - ful and tri - umph - ant, O
1. Ad - es - te fi - de - les, Lae - ti tri - um - phan - tes, Ve -
2. ___ Sing choirs of An - gels, Sing in ex - ul - ta - tion, -

come ye O come - ye to Beth - le - hem;
ni - te ve - ni - te in Beth - le - hem;
Sing all ye cit - i - zens of heav'n - a - bove;

Come and be - hold Him, Born the King of An - gels: O
Na - tum vi - de - te, Re - gem an - ge - lo - rum; Ve
Glo - ry to God - in - the - high - est: O

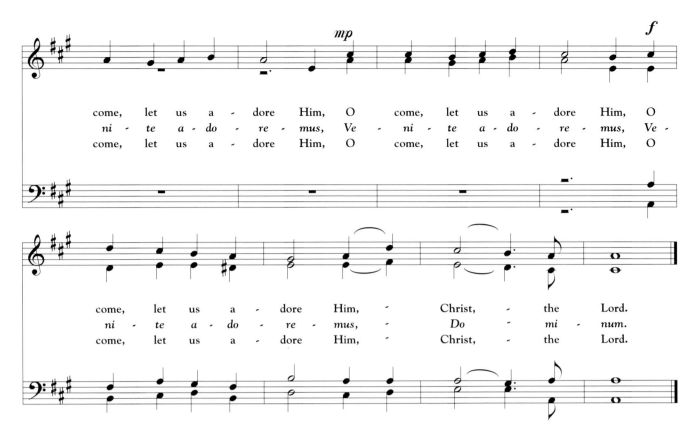

come, let us a - dore Him, O come, let us a - dore Him, O
ni - te a - do - re - mus, Ve - ni - te a - do - re - mus, Ve -
come, let us a - dore Him, O come, let us a - dore Him, O

come, let us a - dore Him, - Christ, - the Lord.
ni - te a - do - re - mus, - Do - mi - num.
come, let us a - dore Him, - Christ, - the Lord.

The Gift of the Magi

O. Henry

One dollar and eighty-seven cents. That was all. And sixty cents of it was in pennies. Pennies saved one and two at a time by bulldozing the grocer and the vegetable man and the butcher until one's cheeks burned with the silent imputation of parsimony that such close dealing implied. Three times Della counted it. One dollar and eighty-seven cents. And the next day would be Christmas.

There was clearly nothing to do but flop down on the shabby little couch and howl. So Della did it. Which instigates the moral reflection that life is made of sobs, sniffles, and smiles, with sniffles predominating.

While the mistress of the home is gradually subsiding from the first stage to the second, take a look at the home. A furnished flat at $8 per week. It did not exactly beggar description, but it certainly had that word on the lookout for the mendicancy squad.

In the vestibule below was a letter-box into which no letter would go, and an electric button from which no mortal finger could coax a ring. Also appertaining thereunto was a card bearing the name "Mr. James Dillingham Young."

The "Dillingham" had been flung to the breeze during a former period of prosperity when its possessor was being paid $30 per week. Now, when the income was shrunk to $20, the letters of "Dillingham" looked blurred, as though they were thinking seriously of contracting to a modest and unassuming D. But whenever Mr. James Dillingham Young came home and reached his flat above he was called "Jim" and greatly hugged by Mrs. James Dillingham Young, already introduced to you as Della. Which is all very good.

Della finished her cry and attended to her cheeks with the powder rag. She stood by the window and looked out dully at a grey cat walking a grey fence in a grey backyard. Tomorrow would be Christmas Day, and she had only $1.87 with which to buy Jim a present. She had been saving every penny she could for months, with this result. Twenty dollars a week doesn't go far. Expenses had been greater than she had calculated. They always are. Only $1.87 to buy a present for Jim. Her Jim. Many a happy hour she had spent planning for something nice for him. Something fine and rare and sterling—something just a little bit near to being worthy of the honour of being owned by Jim.

There was a pier-glass between the windows of the room. Perhaps you have seen a pier-glass in an $8 flat. A very thin and very agile person may, by observing his reflection in a rapid sequence of longitudinal strips, obtain a fairly accurate conception of his looks. Della, being slender, had mastered the art.

Suddenly she whirled from the window and stood before the glass. Her eyes were shining brilliantly, but her face had lost its colour within twenty seconds. Rapidly she pulled down her hair and let it fall to its full length.

Now, there were two possessions of the James Dillingham Youngs in which they both took a mighty pride. One was Jim's gold watch that had been his father's and his grandfather's. The other was Della's hair. Had the Queen of Sheba lived in the flat across the airshaft, Della would have let her hair hang out the window some day to dry just to depreciate Her Majesty's jewels and gifts. Had King Solomon been the janitor, with all his treasures piled up in the basement, Jim would have pulled out his watch every time he passed, just to see him pluck at his beard from envy.

So now Della's beautiful hair fell about her, rippling and shining like a cascade of brown waters. It reached below her knee and made itself almost a garment for her. And then she did it up again nervously and quickly. Once she faltered for a minute and stood still while a tear or two splashed on the worn red carpet.

On went her old brown jacket; on went her old brown hat. With a whirl of skirts and with the brilliant sparkle still in her eyes, she fluttered out the door and down the stairs to the street.

Where she stopped the sign read: "Mme Sofronie. Hair Goods of All Kinds." One flight up Della ran, and collected herself, panting. Madame, large, too white, chilly, hardly looked the "Sofronie."

"Will you buy my hair?" asked Della.

"I buy hair," said Madame. "Take yer hat off and let's have a sight at the looks of it."

Down rippled the brown cascade.

"Twenty dollars," said Madame, lifting the mass with a practised hand.

"Give it to me quick," said Della.

Oh, and the next two hours tripped by on rosy wings. Forget the hashed metaphor. She was ransacking the stores for Jim's present.

She found it at last. It surely had been made for Jim and no one else. There was no other like it in any of the stores, and she had turned all of them inside out. It was a platinum fob chain simple and chaste in design, properly proclaiming its value by substance alone and not by meretricious ornamentation—as all good things should do. It was even worthy of The Watch. As soon as she saw it she knew that it must be Jim's. It was like him. Quietness and value—the description applied to both. Twenty-one dollars they took from her for it, and she hurried home with the 87 cents. With that chain on his watch Jim might be properly anxious about the time in any company. Grand as the watch was, he sometimes looked at it on the sly on account of the old leather strap that he used in place of a chain.

When Della reached home her intoxication gave way a little to prudence and reason. She got out her curling irons and lighted the gas and went to work repairing the ravages made by generosity added to love. Which is always a tremendous task, dear friends—a mammoth task.

Within forty minutes her head was covered with tiny, close-lying curls that made her look wonderfully like a truant schoolboy. She looked at her reflection in the mirror long, carefully, and critically.

"If Jim doesn't kill me," she said to herself, "before he takes a second look at me, he'll say I look like a Coney Island chorus girl. But what could I do—oh! what could I do with a dollar and eighty-seven cents?"

At 7 o'clock the coffee was made and the frying-pan was on the back of the stove, hot and ready to cook the chops.

Jim was never late. Della doubled the fob chain in her hand and sat on the corner of the table near the door that he always entered. Then she heard his step on the stair away down on the first flight, and she turned white for just a moment. She had a habit of saying little silent prayers about the simplest everyday things, and now she whispered: "Please God, make him think I am still pretty."

The door opened and Jim stepped in and closed it. He looked thin and very serious. Poor fellow, he was only twenty-two—and to be burdened with a family! He needed a new overcoat and he was without gloves.

Jim stopped inside the door, as immovable as a setter at the scent of quail. His eyes were fixed upon Della, and there was an expression in them that she could not read, and it terrified her. It was not anger, nor surprise, nor disapproval, nor horror, nor any of the sentiments that she had been prepared for. He simply stared at her fixedly with that peculiar expression on his face.

Della wriggled off the table and went for him.

"Jim, darling," she cried, "don't look at me that way. I had my hair cut off and sold it because I couldn't have lived through Christmas without giving you a present. It'll grow out again—you won't mind, will you? I just had to do it. My hair grows awfully fast. Say 'Merry Christmas!' Jim, and let's be happy. You don't know what a nice—what a beautiful, nice gift I've got for you."

"You've cut off your hair?" asked Jim, laboriously, as if he had not arrived at that patent fact yet even after the hardest mental labour.

"Cut it off and sold it," said Della. "Don't you like me just as well, anyhow? I'm me without my hair, ain't I?"

Jim looked about the room curiously.

"You say your hair is gone?" he said, with an air almost of idiocy.

"You needn't look for it," said Della. "It's sold, I tell you—sold and gone, too. It's Christmas Eve, boy. Be good to me, for it went for you. Maybe the

hairs of my head were numbered," she went on with a sudden serious sweetness, "but nobody could ever count my love for you. Shall I put the chops on, Jim?"

Out of his trance Jim seemed quickly to wake. He enfolded his Della. For ten seconds let us regard with discreet scrutiny some inconsequential object in the other direction. Eight dollars a week or a million a year— what is the difference? A mathematician or a wit would give you the wrong answer. The magi brought valuable gifts, but that was not among them. This dark assertion will be illuminated later on.

Jim drew a package from his overcoat pocket and threw it upon the table.

"Don't make any mistake, Dell," he said, "about me. I don't think there's anything in the way of a haircut or a shave or a shampoo that could make me like my girl any less. But if you'll unwrap that package you may see why you had me going a while at first."

White fingers and nimble tore at the string and paper. And then an ecstatic scream of joy; and then, alas! a quick feminine change to hysterical tears and wails, necessitating the immediate employment of all the comforting powers of the lord of the flat.

For there lay The Combs—the set of combs, side and back, that Della had worshipped for long in a Broadway window. Beautiful combs, pure tortoise shell, with jewelled rims—just the shade to wear in the beautiful vanished hair. They were expensive combs, she knew, and her heart had simply craved and yearned over them without the least hope of possession. And now, they were hers, but the tresses that should have adorned the coveted adornments were gone.

But she hugged them to her bosom, and at length she was able to look up with dim eyes and a smile and say: "My hair grows so fast, Jim!"

And then Della leaped up like a little singed cat and cried, "Oh, oh!"

Jim had not yet seen his beautiful present. She held it out to him eagerly upon her open palm. The dull precious metal seemed to flash with a reflection of her bright and ardent spirit.

"Isn't it a dandy, Jim? I hunted all over town to find it. You'll have to look at the time a hundred times a day now. Give me your watch. I want to see how it looks on it."

Instead of obeying, Jim tumbled down on the couch and put his hands under the back of his head and smiled.

"Dell," said he, "let's put our Christmas presents away and keep 'em a while. They're too nice to use just at present. I sold the watch to get the money to buy your combs. And now suppose you put the chops on."

The magi, as you know, were wise men—wonderfully wise men—who brought gifts to the Babe in the manger. They invented the art of giving Christmas presents. Being wise, their gifts were no doubt wise ones, possibly bearing the privilege of exchange in case of duplication. And here I have lamely related to you the uneventful chronicle of two foolish children in a flat who most unwisely sacrificed for each other the greatest treasures of their house. But in a last word to the wise of these days let it be said that of all who give gifts these two were the wisest. Of all who give and receive gifts, such as they are wisest. Everywhere they are wisest. They are the magi.

The Oxen

Thomas Hardy

Christmas Eve, and twelve of the clock.
   "Now they are all on their knees,"
An elder said as we sat in a flock
   By the embers in hearthside ease.

We pictured the meek mild creatures where
   They dwelt in their strawy pen,
Nor did it occur to one of us there
   To doubt they were kneeling then.

So fair a fancy few would weave
   In these years! Yet, I feel,
If someone said on Christmas Eve,
   "Come; see the oxen kneel

"In the lonely barton by yonder coomb
   Our childhood used to know,"
I should go with him in the gloom,
   Hoping it might be so.

A Visit from St. Nicholas

Clement C. Moore

'Twas the night before Christmas, when all
    through the house
Not a creature was stirring, not even a mouse;
The stockings were hung by the chimney with
    care,
In hopes that St. Nicholas soon would be
    there;
The children were nestled all snug in their beds,
While visions of sugar-plums danced in their
    heads;
And Mamma in her kerchief, and I in my cap,
Had just settled our brains for a long winter's
    nap,
When out on the lawn there arose such a clatter,
I sprang from the bed to see what was the
    matter.
Away to the window I flew like a flash,
Tore open the shutters and threw up the sash.
The moon on the breast of the newfallen snow
Gave the lustre of mid-day to objects below,
When what to my wondering eyes should ap-
    pear,
But a miniature sleigh, and eight tiny reindeer,
With a little old driver, so lively and quick,
I knew in a moment it must be St. Nick.

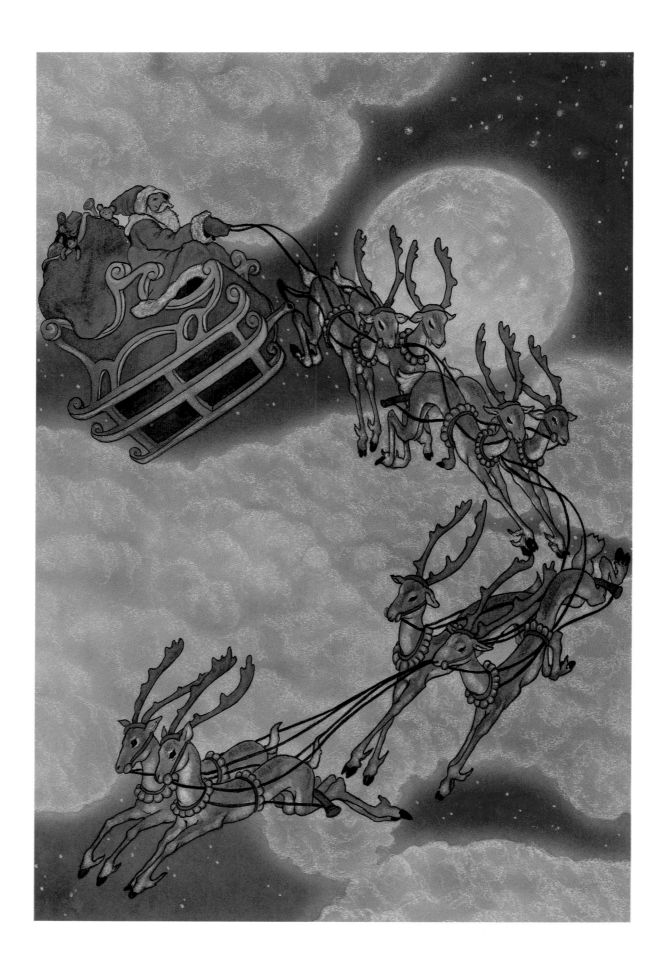

More rapid than eagles his coursers they came,
And he whistled, and shouted, and called them
   by name;
"Now, *Dasher!* now, *Dancer!* now, *Prancer* and
   Vixen!
On, *Comet!* on, *Cupid!* on, *Donder* and *Blitzen!*
To the top of the porch! to the top of the wall!
Now dash away! dash away! dash away all!"
As dry leaves that before the wild hurricane fly,
When they meet with an obstacle, mount to the
   sky,
So up to the house-top the coursers they flew,
With the sleigh full of toys, and St. Nicholas
   too.
And then, in a twinkling, I heard on the roof
The prancing and pawing of each little hoof.
As I drew in my head, and was turning around,
Down the chimney St. Nicholas came with a
   bound.

He was dressed all in fur, from his head to his
    foot,
And his clothes were all tarnished with ashes
    and soot;
A bundle of toys he had flung on his back,
And he looked like a peddler just opening his
    pack.
His eyes—how they twinkled! his dimples how
    merry!
His cheeks were like roses, his nose like a
    cherry!
His droll little mouth was drawn up like a bow,
And the beard of his chin was as white as the
    snow;
The stump of a pipe he held tight in his teeth,
And the smoke it encircled his head like a
    wreath;
He had a broad face and a little round belly,
That shook, when he laughed, like a bowlful of
    jelly.
He was chubby and plump, a right jolly old elf,
And I laughed when I saw him, in spite of
    myself;
A wink of his eye and a twist of his head,
Soon gave me to know I had nothing to dread;
He spoke not a word, but went straight to his
    work,
And filled all the stockings; then turned with a
    jerk,
And laying his finger aside of his nose
And giving a nod, up the chimney he rose;
He sprang to his sleigh, to his team gave a
    whistle,
And away they all flew like the down of a thistle,
But I heard him exclaim, ere he drove out of
    sight,
"Happy Christmas to all, and to all a good-
    night."

A Christmas Carol

Christina Rossetti

In the bleak mid-winter
   Frosty wind made moan,
Earth stood hard as iron,
   Water like a stone;
Snow had fallen, snow on snow,
   Snow on snow,
In the bleak mid-winter
   Long ago.

Our God, Heaven cannot hold Him
   Nor earth sustain;
Heaven and earth shall flee away
   When He comes to reign:
In the bleak mid-winter
   A stable-place sufficed
The Lord God Almighty
   Jesus Christ.

Enough for Him, whom cherubim
   Worship night and day,
A breastful of milk
   And a mangerful of hay;
Enough for Him, whom angels
   Fall down before,
The ox and ass and camel
   Which adore.

Angels and archangels
    May have gathered there,
Cherubim and seraphim
    Thronged the air;
But only His mother
    In her maiden bliss
Worshipped the Beloved
    With a kiss.

What can I give Him
    Poor as I am?
If I were a shepherd
    I would bring a lamb,
If I were a Wise Man
    I would do my part,—
Yet what I can I give Him,
    Give my heart.

Hark! The Herald Angels Sing

Triumphantly

1. Hark! the her - ald an - gels sing, — "Glo - ry to the new - born King,
2. Christ, by high - est heav'n a - dored, — Christ, the ev - er - last - ing Lord;

Peace on earth, and mer - cy mild, — God and sin - ners
Late in time be - hold Him come, — — Off - spring of the

re - con - ciled." Joy - ful, all ye na - tions rise, — Join the tri - umph
fa - vored one. Veiled in flesh, the God - head see! — Hail, th'in - car - nate

42

of the skies; - With th'an - gel - ic host pro - claim, "Christ is - born in
De - i - ty! - Pleased as man with man to dwell, Je - sus, - our Em -

Beth - le - hem." Hark! the her - ald an - gels sing, "Glo - ry - to the new - born King."
man - u - el. Hark! the her - ald an - gels sing, "Glo - ry - to the new - born King."

The Little Match Girl

Hans Christian Andersen

It was terribly cold; it was snowing and almost dark. It was also the last evening of the year. In the cold and darkness a poor little girl, with bare head and naked feet, went along the streets. When she had left home, it is true, she had had slippers on, but what good were they? They were very large; big enough for her mother to wear. The little girl lost them as she hurried across the street to get out of the way of two carts driving furiously along. One slipper was not to be found again, and a boy had picked up the other and had run away with it. He said he could use it for a cradle when he had children of his own! So the little girl had to go walking in her bare feet, which were blue with cold. She carried a lot of matches in an old apron and a box of them in her hand. No one had bought any from her the whole day; no one had given her so much as a penny.

Hungry and shivering, she went along, poor little thing, a picture of misery.

The snowflakes fell on her long yellow hair that curled so prettily on her neck, but she did not think of that now. Lights were shining in all the windows, and there was a tempting smell of roast goose, for it was New Year's Eve. Yes, she was thinking of that.

In a corner formed by two houses, one of which projected a little beyond the other, she sat down and huddled against the cold. She had tucked her feet under her, but she felt colder and colder. She didn't dare go home, for she had not sold any matches nor earned a single penny, and her father would beat her. Anyway, it was cold at home: they had only the roof above them, through which the wind whistled, although the largest cracks had been stopped up with straw and rags.

Her hands were almost dead with cold. Ah! One little match might do her good! If she dared take only one out of the box, strike it on the wall, and warm her fingers! She took one out and struck it. How it sputtered and burned!

It was a warm, bright flame, like a little candle, when she held her hands over it. It was a wonderful little light, and it really seemed to the child as though she were sitting in front of a great iron stove with polished brass feet and brass ornaments. How the fire burned, and how it warmed! But what was that? The little girl was already stretching out her feet to warm them too, when—out went the little flame, the stove vanished, and she had only the remains of the burned match in her hand.

She struck a second one on the wall; it burned and gave a light, and where the light fell on the wall it became transparent, like a veil—she could see right into the room. A white tablecloth was spread upon the table, which was decked with shining china dishes, and there was a lovely smell of roast goose stuffed with apples and prunes. What pleased the poor little girl more than anything was that the goose hopped down from the dish and came waddling across the floor straight towards her. Just at that moment, out went the match, and only the thick, cold wall was to be seen. So she lighted another match. And there she was sitting under the beautiful Christmas tree; it was much larger and more decorated than the one she had seen through the glass doors at the rich merchant's. The green boughs were lit up with thousands of candles, and gaily painted figures, like those in the shop windows, looked down on her. The little girl stretched her hands out towards them and—out went the match. The Christmas candles rose higher and higher, till they were only the stars in the sky; one of them fell, leaving a long fiery trail behind it.

"Now, someone is dying," said the little girl, for her old grandmother, the only person who had ever been good to her and who was now dead, had said that when a star falls a soul goes up to heaven.

She struck another match on the wall; it lighted immediately and in its glow stood her old grandmother, so dazzling and bright, and so kind and loving.

"Grandmother!" cried the little girl. "Oh, please take me with you! I know that you will go away when the match goes out; you will vanish like the warm stove and the beautiful roast goose and the lovely big Christmas tree."

She quickly lighted the whole box of matches, for she did not wish to let her grandmother go. The matches burned with such a blaze that it was lighter than day, and the old grandmother had never appeared so beautiful or so tall before. Taking the little girl in her arms she flew up with her in brightness and joy, high, so high; and there was no cold, or hunger, or sorrow—for they were with God.

But in the corner by the houses, in the cold dawn, the little girl was still sitting, with red cheeks and a smile on her lips—frozen to death on the last evening of the old year. The new year's sun shone down on the little body. The child sat up stiffly, holding her matches, of which a box had been burned.

"She must have tried to warm herself," someone said.

No one knew what beautiful things she had seen, nor into what glory she had entered with her grandmother on the joyous New Year.

An Alphabet of Christmas

Anonymous

A for the Animals out in the stable.

B for the Babe in their manger for cradle.

C for the Carols so blithe and gay.

D for December, the twenty-fifth day.

E for the Eve when we're all so excited.

F for the Fire when the Yule Log is lighted.

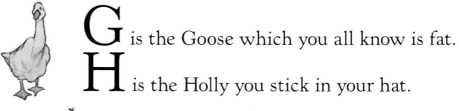

G is the Goose which you all know is fat.

H is the Holly you stick in your hat.

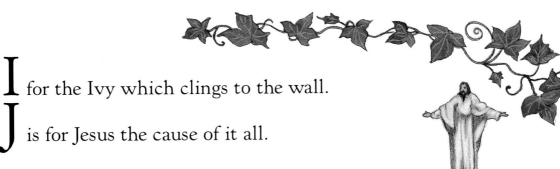

I for the Ivy which clings to the wall.

J is for Jesus the cause of it all.

K for the Kindness begot by this feast.

L is the Light shining way in the East.

M for the Mistletoe. Beware where it hangs!

N is the Nowell the angels first sang.

O for the Oxen, the first to adore Him.

P for the Presents wise men laid before Him.

Q for the Queerness that this should have been,
near two thousand years before you were seen.

R for the Romps and the Raisins and Nuts.

S for the Stockings that Santa Claus stuffs.

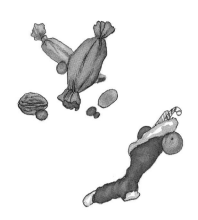

T for the Toys on the Christmas Tree hanging.

U is for Us over all the world ranging.

V for the Visitors welcomed so warmly.

W for the Waits at your door singing heartily!

bother me! all I can say,

Is this is the end of my Christmas lay.

So now to you all, wherever you may be,

A merry merry Christmas, and may many you see!

Christmas Greeting from a Fairy to a Child

Lewis Carroll

Lady, dear, if Fairies may
   For a moment lay aside
Cunning tricks and elfish play,
   'Tis at happy Christmas-tide.

We have heard the children say—
   Gentle children, whom we love—
Long ago on Christmas Day,
   Came a message from above.

Still, as Christmas-tide comes round,
   They remember it again—
Echo still the joyful sound
   "Peace on earth, good-will to men!"

Yet the hearts must childlike be
   Where such heavenly guests abide;
Unto children, in their glee,
   All the year is Christmas-tide!

Thus, forgetting tricks and play
   For a moment, Lady dear,
We would wish you, if we may,
   Merry Christmas, glad New Year!

The Year Santa Came Late

Willa Cather

This is a tale of the bleak, bitter Northland, where the frost is eternal and the snows never melt, where the wide white plains stretch for miles and miles . . . and where the Heavens at night are made terribly beautiful by the trembling flashes of the northern lights, and the green icebergs float in stately grandeur down the dark currents of the hungry polar sea. . . . The only cheerful thing about all this country is that far up within the Arctic Circle, just on the edge of the boundless snow plains, there is a big house . . . where lights shine all year round from the windows, and the wide halls are warmed by blazing fires. For this is the house of his beloved Saintship, Nicholas, whom the children the world over call Santa Claus.

Now every child knows this house is beautiful, and beautiful it is, for it is one of the most home-like places in the world. Just inside the front door is the big hall, where every evening after his work is done Santa Claus sits by the roaring fire and chats with his wife, Mamma Santa, and the White Bear. Then there is the dining room, and the room where Papa and Mamma Santa sleep, and to the rear are the workshops, where all the wonderful toys are made, and last of all the White Bear's sleeping room, for the White Bear has to sleep in a bed of clean white snow every night, and so his room is away from the heated part of the house.

But most boys and girls do not know much about the White Bear, for, though he is really a very important personage, he has been strangely neglected by the biographers of Santa Claus. . . . He is not at all like the bears who carry off naughty children, and does not even belong to the same family as the bears who ate up the forty children who mocked at the

Prophet's bald head. On the contrary, this bear is a most gentle and kindly fellow, and fonder of boys and girls than any one else in the world, except Santa Claus himself. He has lived with Papa Santa from time immemorial, helping him in his workshop, painting rocking horses, and stretching drum heads, and gluing yellow wigs on doll babies. But his principal duty is to care for the reindeer, those swift, strong, nervous little beasts, without whom the hobby horses and dolls and red drums would never reach the little children in the world.

One evening, on the twenty-third of December—the rest of the date does not matter—Papa Santa sat by the fire in the great hall, blowing the smoke from his nostrils, until his ruddy round face shone through it like a full moon through the mist. He was in a happier mood even than usual, for his long year's work in his shop was done, the last nail had been driven, the last coat of paint had dried. All the vast array of toys stood ready to go into the sealskin bags and be piled into the sleigh for the children of the world.

Opposite him sat Mamma Santa, putting the last dainty stitches on a doll dress for a little sick girl somewhere down in the world. Mamma Santa

never kept track of where the different children lived; Papa Santa and the White Bear attended to the address book. It was enough for her to know that they were children and good children, she didn't care to know any more. By her chair sat the White Bear, eating his dog sausage. The White Bear was always hungry between meals, and Mamma Santa always kept a plate of his favorite sausage ready for him in the pantry, which, as there was no fire there, was a refrigerator as well.

As Papa Santa bent to light his pipe once again, he spoke to the White Bear:

"The reindeer are all in good shape, are they? You've seen them tonight? There are no problems?"

"I gave them their feed and rubbed them down an hour ago, and I never saw them friskier. They ought to skim like birds tomorrow night. As I came away, though, I thought I saw the Were-Wolf Dog hanging around, so I locked up the stable."

"That was right," said Papa Santa, approvingly. "He was there for no good, depend on that. Last year he tampered with the harness and cut it so that four traces broke before I reached Norway."

Mamma Santa sent her needle through the fine cambric she was stitching with an indignant thrust, and spoke so emphatically that the little white curls under her cap bobbed about her face. "I cannot understand the perverse wickedness of that animal, nor what he has against you, that he should be forever troubling you, or against those World-Children, poor little innocents, that he should be forever trying to defraud them of their Christmas presents. He is certainly the meanest animal from here to the Pole."

"That he is," said Papa Santa, "and there is no reason for it at all. But he hates everything that is not mean as himself."

"I am sure, Papa, that he will never be at rest until he has brought about some serious accident. Hadn't the Bear better look about the stables again?"

"I'll sleep there tonight and watch, if you say so," said the White Bear, rapping the floor with his shaggy tail.

"O, there is no need of that, we must all get our sleep tonight, for we have hard work and a long journey before us tomorrow. I can trust the reindeer pretty well to look after themselves. Come, Mamma, come, we must get to bed." Papa Santa shook the ashes out of his pipe and blew out the lights, and the White Bear went to stretch himself in his clean white snow.

When all was quiet about the house, there stole from out the shadow of the wall a great dog, shaggy and monstrous to look upon. His hair was red, and his eyes were bright, like ominous fires . . . and there was always a little foam about his lips as though he were raging with some inward fury. He carried his tail between his legs, for he was as cowardly as he was vicious. This was the wicked Were-Wolf Dog who hated everything; the beasts and the birds and Santa Claus and the White Bear, and most of all the little children of the world. Nothing made him so angry as to think that there really are good children in the world, little children who love each other, and are simple and gentle and fond of everything that lives, whether it breathes or blooms. For years he had been trying in one way and another to delay Santa Claus' journey so that the children would get no beautiful gifts from him at Christmastime. For the Were-Wolf Dog hated Christmas too, incomprehensible as that may seem. He was thoroughly wicked and evil, and Christmastime is the birthday of Goodness, and every year on Christmas Eve the rage in his dark heart burned anew.

He stole softly to the window of the stable, and peered in where the swift, tiny reindeer stood each in his warm little stall, pawing the ground impatiently. For on glorious moonlight nights like that the reindeer never slept, they were so homesick for their freedom and their wide white snow plains.

"Little reindeer," called the Were-Wolf Dog, softly, and all the little reindeer pricked up their ears. "Little reindeer, it is a lovely night," and all the little reindeer sighed softly. They knew, ah, how well they knew!

"Little reindeer, the moon is shining as brightly as the sun does in the summer; the North wind is blowing fresh and cold, driving the little clouds across the sky like white sea birds. The snow is just hard enough to bear without breaking, and your brothers are running like wild things over its white crust. And the stars, ah, the stars, little brothers, they gleam like a million jewels, and glitter like icicles all over the face of the sky. Come, see how they sparkle."

The reindeer stamped impatiently in their little stalls. It was very hard. They wanted to be out racing freely with all the other reindeer.

"Come, little reindeer, let me tell you why all your brothers run toward the Polar Sea tonight. It is because tonight the northern lights will flash as they never did before, and the great streaks of red and purple and violet will shoot across the sky until all the people of the world shall see them, who never saw before. Listen, little reindeer, it is just the night for a run, a long free run, with no traces to tangle your feet and no sleigh to drag. Come, let us go, you will be back again by dawn and no one will ever know."

Dunder stamped in his stall, it made him long to be gone, to hear what the Were-Wolf Dog said. "No, no, we cannot, for tomorrow we must start with the toys for the little children of the world."

"But you will be back tomorrow. Just when the dim light is touching the tops of the icebergs and making the fresh snow red, you will be speeding home. Ah, it will be a glorious run, and you will see the lights as they never shone before. Do you not pant to feel the wind about you, little reindeer?"

Then Cupid and Blitzen could withstand his enticing words no longer, and begged, "Come, Dunder, let us go tonight. It has been so long since we have seen the lights, and we will be back tomorrow."

Now the reindeer knew well enough they ought not to go, but reindeer are not like people, and sometimes the things they want most awfully to do are the very things that they ought not to do. The thought of the fresh winds and their dear lights of the North and the moonlight snow drove them wild, for the reindeer love their freedom more than any other animal, and swift motion, and the free winds.

So the dog pried open the door, with the help of the reindeer forcing it from within, and they all dashed out into the clear moonlight and scurried away toward the North like gleeful rabbits. "We will be back by morning," said Cupid. "We will be back," said Dunder. And, poor little reindeer, they loved the snow so well that it scarcely seemed wrong to go.

O, how fine it was to feel that wind in their fur again! They tossed their antlers in the fresh wind, and their tiny hoofs rang on the hard snow as they ran. They ran for miles and miles without growing tired, or losing their first pleasure in it. . . .

"Slower, slower, little reindeer, for I must lead the way. You will not find the place where the beasts are assembled," called the Were-Wolf Dog.

The little reindeer could no more go slowly than a boy can when the fire engines dash by. So they got the Were-Wolf Dog in the center of the pack and fairly bore him on with them. On they ran over those vast plains of snow that sparkled as brightly as the sky did above, and Dasher and Prancer bellowed aloud with glee. At last there lay before them the boundless stretch of the Polar Sea. Dark and silent it was, as mysterious as the strange secret of the Pole which it guards forever. Here and there where the ice floes had parted showed a crevice of black water, and the great walls of ice glittered like flame when the northern lights flung their red banners across the sky, and tipped the icebergs with fire. There the reindeer paused a moment for very joy, and the Were-Wolf Dog fell behind silently.

"Is the ice safe, old dog?" asked Vixen, calling to the Were-Wolf Dog.

"To the right it is, off and away, little reindeer. It is growing late," said the Were-Wolf Dog, shouting hoarsely; "To the right."

And the heedless little reindeer dashed on, never noticing that the wicked Were-Wolf Dog stayed behind on the shore. Now when they were out a good way upon the sea they heard a frightful cracking grinding sound, such as the ice makes when it breaks up.

"To the shore, little brothers, to the shore!" cried Dunder, but it was too late. The wicked Were-Wolf Dog where he stood on the land saw the treacherous ice break and part, and the head of every little reindeer go down under the black water. Then he turned and fled over the snow, with his tail tighter between his legs than ever, for he was too cowardly to look upon his own evil work.

As for the reindeer, the black current caught them and whirled them down under the ice, all but Dunder and Dasher and Prancer, who at last rose to the surface and lifted their heads above the water.

"Swim, little brothers, we may yet make the shore," cried Dunder. So among the cakes of broken ice that cut them at every stroke, the three brave little beasts began to struggle toward the shore that seemed so far away. A great chunk of ice struck Prancer in the breast, and he groaned and sank. Then Dasher began to breathe heavily and fell behind, and when Dunder stayed to help him he said, "No, no, little brother, I cannot make it. You must not try to help me, or we will both go down. Go tell it all to the White Bear. Goodbye, little brother, we will skim the white snow fields no more together." And with that he, too, sank down into the black water, and Dunder struggled on all alone.

When at last he dragged himself wearily upon the shore he was ex-
hausted and cruelly cut and bleeding. But there was no time to be lost.
Spent and suffering as he was, he set out across the plains.

Late in the night the White Bear heard someone tapping, tapping
against his window and saw poor Dunder standing there all covered with
ice and blood.

"Come out, brother," he gasped, "the others are all dead and drowned,
only I am left. . . ."

Then the White Bear hastened out . . . and Dunder told him all about
the cruel treachery of the Were-Wolf Dog.

"Alas," cried the White Bear, "and who shall tell Santa of this, and who
will drag his sleigh tomorrow to carry the gifts to the little children of the
world? Empty will their stockings hang on Christmas morning, and
Santa's heart will be broken."

Then poor Dunder sank down in the snow and wept.

"Do not despair, Dunder. We must go tonight to the ice hummock where
the beasts meet to begin their Christmas revels. Can you run a little longer,
poor reindeer?"

"I will run until I die," said Dunder, bravely. "Get on my back and we
will go." . . . And they sped away to the great ice hummock where the
animals of the North all gather to keep their Christmas.

The ice hummock is a great pile of ice and snow right under the North
Star, and all the animals were there drinking punches and wishing each

other a Merry Christmas. There were seals, and fur otters, and white ermines, and whales, and bears, and many strange birds, and the tawny Lapland dogs that are as strong as horses. But the Were-Wolf Dog was not there. The White Bear paid no heed to any of them, but climbed up to the very top of the huge ice hummock. Then he stood up and cried out:

"Animals of the North, listen to me!" and all the animals ceased from their merrymaking and looked up to the ice hummock where the White Bear stood, looking very strange up there, all alone in the starlight.

"Listen to me," thundered the White Bear, "and I will tell you such a tale of wickedness and treachery as never came up among us before. This night the wicked Were-Wolf Dog . . . came to the reindeer of Santa Claus and with enticing words lured them northward, promising to show them the great lights as they never shone before. But black Death he showed them, and the bottom of the Polar Sea." Then he showed them poor bleeding Dunder, and told how all the tiny reindeer had been drowned and all the treachery of the Were-Wolf Dog. . . .

"Now, O animals," the White Bear went on, "who among you will go back with me and draw the sleigh full of presents down to the little World-Children, for a shame would it be to all of us if they should awaken and find themselves forgotten and their stockings empty."

But none of the animals replied. . . .

"What," cried the White Bear. "Is there not one of you who will . . . take the place of our brothers who are now dead? . . ."

But the animals all thought of the wide plains and the stinging North wind and their scampers of old, and hung their heads and were silent. Poor Dunder groaned aloud, and even the White Bear had begun to despair, when there spoke up a poor old seal with but one fin, for he had fallen into the seal fishers' hands and been maimed. . . . "I am only an old seal who has been twice wounded by the hunters, and am a cripple, but lo, I myself will go with the White Bear, and though I can travel but a mile a day at best, yet will I hobble on my tail and my one fin until I have dragged the sleigh full of presents to the World-Children."

Then the animals were all ashamed of themselves, and the reindeer all sprang forward and cried, "We will go, take us!"

So the next day, a little later than usual, Santa Claus wrapped himself in his fur lap robes, and seven new reindeer, headed by Dunder, flew like the winged wind toward the coast of Norway. And if any of you remember getting your presents a little late that year, it was because the new reindeer were not used to their work yet, though they tried hard enough.

The Fir-Tree

Hans Christian Andersen

There was once a pretty little fir-tree in a wood. It was in a capital position, for it could get sun, and there was enough air, and all around grew many tall companions, both pines and firs. The little fir-tree's greatest desire was to grow up. It did not heed the warm sun and the fresh air, or notice the little peasant children who ran about chattering when they came out to gather wild strawberries and raspberries. Often they found a whole basketful and strung strawberries on a straw; they would sit down by the little fir-tree and say, "What a pretty little one this is!" The tree did not like that at all.

By the next year it had grown a whole ring taller, and the year after that another ring more, for you can always tell a fir-tree's age from its rings.

"Oh! if I were only a great tree like the others!" sighed the little fir-tree, "then I could stretch out my branches far and wide and look out into the great world! The birds would build their nests in my branches, and when the wind blew I would bow to it politely just like the others!" It took no pleasure in the sunshine, nor in the birds, nor in the rose-coloured clouds that sailed over it at dawn and at sunset. Then the winter came, and the snow lay white and sparkling all around, and a hare would come and spring right over the little fir-tree, which annoyed it very much. But when two more winters had passed the fir-tree was so tall that the hare had to run around it. "Ah! to grow and grow, and become great and old! that is the only pleasure in life," thought the tree. In the autumn the woodcutters used to come and hew some of the tallest trees; this happened every year, and the young fir-tree would shiver as the magnificent trees fell crashing and crackling to the ground, their branches hewn off, and the great trunks left bare, so that they were almost unrecognisable. But then they were laid on wagons and dragged out of the wood by horses. "Where are they going? What will happen to them?"

In spring, when the swallows and storks came, the fir-tree asked them, "Do you know where they were taken? Have you met them?"

The swallows knew nothing of them, but the stork nodded his head thoughtfully, saying, "I think I know. I met many new ships as I flew from Egypt; there were splendid masts on the ships. I'll wager those were they! They had the scent of fir-trees. Ah! those are grand, grand!"

"Oh! if I were only big enough to sail away over the sea too! What sort of thing is the sea? what does it look like?"

"Oh! it would take much too long to tell you all that," said the stork, and off he went.

"Rejoice in your youth," said the sunbeams, "rejoice in the sweet growing time, in the young life within you."

And the wind kissed it and the dew wept tears over it, but the fir-tree did not understand.

Towards Christmas-time quite little trees were cut down, some not as big as the young fir-tree, or just the same age, and now it had no peace or rest for longing to be away. These little trees, which were chosen for their beauty, kept all their branches; they were put in carts and drawn out of the wood by horses.

"Whither are those going?" asked the fir-tree; "they are no bigger than I, and one there was much smaller even! Why do they keep their branches? Where are they taken to?"

"We know! we know!" twittered the sparrows. "Down there in the city we have peeped in at the windows, we know where they go! They attain to the greatest splendour and magnificence you can imagine! We have looked in at the windows and seen them planted in the middle of the warm room and adorned with the most beautiful things—golden apples, sweetmeats, toys, and hundreds of candles."

"And then?" asked the fir-tree, trembling in every limb with eagerness, "and then? what happens then?"

"Oh, we haven't seen anything more than that. That was simply matchless!"

"Am I too destined to the same brilliant career?" wondered the fir-tree excitedly. "That is even better than sailing over the sea! I am sick with longing. If it were only Christmas! Now I am tall and grown-up like those which were taken away last year. Ah, if I were only in the cart! If I were only in the warm room with all the splendour and magnificence! And then? Then comes something better, something still more beautiful, else why should they dress us up? There must be something greater, something grander to come—but what? Oh! I am pining away! I really don't know what's the matter with me!"

"Rejoice in us," said the air and sunshine, "rejoice in your fresh youth in the free air!"

But it took no notice, and just grew and grew; there it stood fresh and green in winter and in summer, and all who saw it said, "What a beautiful tree!" And at Christmas-time it was the first to be cut down. The axe went deep into the pith; the tree fell to the ground with a groan; it felt bruised and faint. It could not think of happiness, it was sad at leaving its home, the spot where it had sprung up; it knew, too, that it would never see again its dear old companions, or the little shrubs and flowers, perhaps not even the birds. Altogether the parting was not pleasant.

When the tree came to itself again it was packed in a yard with other trees, and a man was saying, "This is a splendid one, we shall only want this."

Then came two footmen in livery and carried the fir-tree into a large and beautiful room. There were pictures hanging upon the walls, and near the Dutch stove stood great Chinese vases with lions on their lids; there were armchairs, silk-covered sofas, big tables laden with picture-books and toys, worth hundreds of pounds—at least, so the children said. The fir-tree was placed in a great tub filled with sand, but no one could see that it was a tub, for it was all hung with greenery and stood on a gay carpet. How the tree trembled! What was coming now? The young ladies and the servants decked it out. On its branches they hung little nets cut out of coloured paper, each full of sugarplums; gilt apples and nuts hung down as if they were growing, and over a hundred red, blue, and white tapers were fastened among the branches. Dolls as life-like as human beings—the fir-tree had never seen any before—were suspended among the green, and right up at the top was fixed a gold tinsel star; it was gorgeous, quite unusually gorgeous!

"To-night," they all said, "to-night it will be lighted!"

"Ah!" thought the tree, "if it were only evening! Then the tapers would soon be lighted. What will happen then? I wonder whether the trees will come from the wood to see me, or if the sparrows will fly against the window panes? Am I to stand here decked out thus through winter and summer?"

It was not a bad guess, but the fir-tree had real bark-ache from sheer longing, and bark-ache in trees is just as bad as head-ache in human beings.

Now the tapers were lighted. What a glitter! What splendour! The tree quivered in all its branches so much, that one of the candles caught the green, and singed it. "Take care!" cried the young ladies, and they extinguished it.

Now the tree did not even dare to quiver. It was really terrible! It was so afraid of losing any of its ornaments, and it was quite bewildered by all the radiance.

And then the folding doors were opened, and a crowd of children rushed in, as though they wanted to knock down the whole tree, whilst the older people followed, soberly. The children stood quite silent, but only for a moment, and then they shouted again, and danced round the tree, and snatched off one present after another.

"What are they doing?" thought the tree. "What is going to happen?" And the tapers burnt low on the branches, and were put out one by one, and then the children were given permission to plunder the tree. They rushed at it so that all its boughs creaked; if it had not been fastened by the gold star at the top to the ceiling, it would have been overthrown.

The children danced about with their splendid toys, and no one looked at the tree, except the old nurse, who came and peeped amongst the boughs, just to see if a fig or an apple had been forgotten.

"A story! a story!" cried the children, and dragged a little stout man to the tree; he sat down beneath it, saying, "Here we are in the greenwood, and the tree will be delighted to listen! But I am only going to tell one story. Shall it be Henny Penny or Humpty Dumpty who fell downstairs, and yet gained great honour and married a princess?"

"Henny Penny!" cried some; "Humpty Dumpty!" cried others; there was a perfect babel of voices! Only the fir-tree kept silent, and thought, "Am I not to be in it? Am I to have nothing to do with it?"

But it had already been in it, and played out its part. And the man told them about Humpty Dumpty who fell downstairs and married a princess. The children clapped their hands and cried, "Another! another!" They wanted the story of Henny Penny also, but they only got Humpty Dumpty. The fir-tree stood quite astonished and thoughtful: the birds in the wood had never related anything like that. "Humpty Dumpty fell downstairs and yet married a princess! yes, that is the way of the world!" thought the tree, and was sure it must be true, because such a nice man had told the story. "Well, who knows? Perhaps I shall fall downstairs and marry a princess." And it rejoiced to think that next day it would be decked out again with candles, toys, glittering ornaments, and fruits. "To-morrow I shall quiver again with excitement. I shall enjoy to the full all my splendour. To-morrow I shall hear Humpty Dumpty again, and perhaps Henny Penny too." And the tree stood silent and lost in thought all through the night.

Next morning the servants came in. "Now the dressing up will begin again," thought the tree. But they dragged it out of the room, and up the stairs to the lumber-room, and put it in a dark corner, where no ray of light could penetrate. "What does this mean?" thought the tree. "What am I to do here? What is there for me to hear?" And it leant against the wall, and thought and thought. And there was time enough for that, for days and nights went by, and no one came; at last when someone did come, it was only to put some great boxes into the corner. Now the tree was quite covered; it seemed as if it had been quite forgotten.

"Now it is winter out-doors," thought the fir-tree. "The ground is hard and covered with snow, they can't plant me yet, and that is why I am staying here under cover till the spring comes. How thoughtful they are! Only I wish it were not so terribly dark and lonely here; not even a little hare! It was so nice out in the wood, when the snow lay all around, and the hare leapt past me; yes, even when he leapt over me: but I didn't like it then. It's so dreadfully lonely up here."

"Squeak, squeak!" said a little mouse, stealing out, followed by a second. They sniffed at the fir-tree, and then crept between its boughs. "It's frightfully cold," said the little mice. "How nice it is to be here! Don't you think so too, you old fir-tree?"

"I'm not at all old," said the tree; "there are many much older than I am."

"Where do you come from?" asked the mice, "and what do you know?" They were extremely inquisitive. "Do tell us about the most beautiful place in the world. Is that where you come from? Have you been in the storeroom, where cheeses lie on the shelves, and hams hang from the ceiling, where one dances on tallow candles, and where one goes in thin and comes out fat?"

"I know nothing about that," said the tree. "But I know the wood, where the sun shines, and the birds sing." And then it told them all about its young days, and the little mice had never heard anything like that before, and they listened with all their ears, and said: "Oh, how much you have seen! How lucky you have been!"

"I?" said the fir-tree, and then it thought over what it had told them. "Yes, on the whole those were very happy times." But then it went on to tell them about Christmas Eve, when it had been adorned with sweet-meats and tapers.

"Oh!" said the little mice, "how lucky you have been, you old fir-tree!"

"I'm not at all old," said the tree. "I only came from the wood this winter. I am only a little backward, perhaps, in my growth."

"How beautifully you tell stories!" said the little mice. And next evening they came with four others, who wanted to hear the tree's story, and it told still more, for it remembered everything so clearly and thought: "Those were happy times! But they may come again. Humpty Dumpty fell downstairs, and yet he married a princess; perhaps I shall also marry a princess!" And then it thought of a pretty little birch-tree that grew out in the wood, and seemed to the fir-tree a real princess, and a very beautiful one too.

"Who is Humpty Dumpty?" asked the little mice.

And then the tree told the whole story; it could remember every single word, and the little mice were ready to leap on to the topmost branch out of sheer joy! Next night many more mice came, and on Sunday even two rats; but they did not care about the story, and that troubled the little mice, for now they thought less of it too.

"Is that the only story you know?" asked the rats.

"The only one," answered the tree. "I heard that on my happiest evening, but I did not realise then how happy I was."

"That's a very poor story. Don't you know one about bacon or tallow candles? a storeroom story?"

"No," said the tree.

"Then we are much obliged to you," said the rats, and they went back to their friends.

At last the little mice went off also, and the tree said, sighing: "Really it was very pleasant when the lively little mice sat round and listened whilst I told them stories. But now that's over too. But now I will think of the time when I shall be brought out again, to keep up my spirits."

But when did that happen? Well, it was one morning when they came to tidy up the lumber-room; the boxes were set aside, and the tree brought out; they threw it really rather roughly on the floor, but a servant dragged it off at once downstairs, where there was daylight once more.

"Now life begins again!" thought the tree. It felt the fresh air, the first rays of the sun, and there it was out in the yard! Everything passed so quickly; the tree quite forgot to notice itself, there was so much to look at

all around. The yard opened on a garden full of flowers; the roses were so fresh and sweet, hanging over a little trellis, the lime-trees were in blossom, and the swallows flew about, saying: "Quirre-virre-vit, my husband has come home;" but it was not the fir-tree they meant.

"Now I shall live," thought the tree joyfully, stretching out its branches wide; but, alas! they were all withered and yellow; and it was lying in a corner among weeds and nettles. The golden star was still on its highest bough, and it glittered in the bright sunlight. In the yard some of the merry children were playing, who had danced so gaily round the tree at Christmas. One of the little ones ran up, and tore off the gold star.

"Look what was left on the ugly old fir-tree!" he cried, and stamped on the boughs so that they cracked under his feet.

And the tree looked at all the splendour and freshness of the flowers in the garden, and then looked at itself, and wished that it had been left lying in the dark corner of the lumber-room; it thought of its fresh youth in the wood, of the merry Christmas Eve, and of the little mice who had listened so happily to the story of Humpty Dumpty.

"Too late! Too late!" thought the old tree. "If only I had enjoyed myself whilst I could. Now all is over and gone."

And a servant came and cut the tree into small pieces, there was quite a bundle of them; they flickered brightly under the great copper in the brew-house; the tree sighed deeply, and each sigh was like a pistol-shot; so the children who were playing there ran up, and sat in front of the fire, gazing at it, and crying, "Piff! puff! bang!" But for each report, which was really a sigh, the tree was thinking of a summer's day in the wood, or of a winter's night out there, when the stars were shining; it thought of Christmas Eve, and of Humpty Dumpty, which was the only story it had heard, or could tell, and then the tree had burnt away.

The children played on in the garden, and the youngest had the golden star on his breast, which the tree had worn on the happiest evening of its life; and now that was past—and the tree had passed away—and the story too, all ended and done with.

And that's the way with all stories!

Christmas is coming

Mother Goose

Christmas is coming, the geese are getting
  fat,
Please to put a penny in an old man's hat;
If you haven't got a penny a ha'penny will do,
If you haven't got a ha'penny, God bless you.

The Celebration
of Christmas

In the Week
When Christmas Comes

Eleanor Farjeon

This is the week when Christmas comes.

Let every pudding burst with plums,
And every tree bear dolls and drums,
 In the week when Christmas comes.

Let every hall have boughs of green,
With berries glowing in between,
 In the week when Christmas comes.

Let every doorstep have a song
Sounding the dark street along,
 In the week when Christmas comes.

Let every steeple ring a bell
With a joyful tale to tell,
    In the week when Christmas comes.

Let every night put forth a star
To show us where the heavens are,
    In the week when Christmas comes.

Let every stable have a lamb
Sleeping warm beside its dam,
    In the week when Christmas comes.

This is the week when Christmas comes.

Deck the Halls

Joyfully

1. Deck the halls with boughs of hol - ly,
2. See the blaz - ing Yule be - fore us,
3. Fast a - way the old year pass - es,
} Fa la la la la, la la la la.

'Tis the sea - son to be jol - ly,
Strike the harp and join the cho - rus,
Hail the new, ye lads and lass - es,
} Fa la la la la, la la la la.

Don we now our gay ap - par - rel,
Fol - low me in mer - ry mea - sure, } Fa la la la la la, la la la.
Sing we joy - ous all to - geth - er,

Troll the an - cient Yule - tide car - ol,
While I tell of Yule - tide trea - sure, } Fa la la la la, la la la la.
Heed - less of the wind and weath - er,

little tree

e. e. cummings

little tree
little silent Christmas tree
you are so little
you are more like a flower

who found you in the green forest
and were you very sorry to come away?
see   i will comfort you
because you smell so sweetly

i will kiss your cool bark
and hug you safe and tight
just as your mother would,
only don't be afraid

look   the spangles
that sleep all the year in a dark box
dreaming of being taken out and allowed to
      shine,
the balls the chains red and gold the fluffy
      threads,

put up your little arms
and I'll give them all to you to hold
every finger shall have its ring
and there won't be a single place dark or
      unhappy

then when you're quite dressed
you'll stand in the window for everyone to
      see
and how they'll stare!
oh but you'll be very proud

and my little sister and i will take hands
and looking up at our beautiful tree
we'll dance and sing
"Noel Noel"

O Christmas Tree

O Tannenbaum

Happily

1. O Christ-mas tree, O Christ-mas tree, For-ev-er green your branch-es!
1. O Tan-nen-baum, O Tan-nen-baum, Wie treu sind dei-ne Blät-ter!
2. And, oh, the Christ-mas tree can be A source of sim-ple plea-sure!

How full and fair in sum-mer's glow, And thick and green in win-ter's snow. O
Du grünst nicht nur zur Som-mers-zeit, Nein, auch im Win-ter, wenn es schneit. O
To ev-ery girl and ev-ery boy It speaks of hol-i-days and joy! Ah

Christ-mas tree, O Christ-mas tree, For-ev-er green your branch-es!
Tan-nen-baum, O Tan-nen-baum, Wie treu sind dei-ne Blät-ter!
yes, the Christ-mas tree can be A source of sim-ple plea-sure.

from *A Child's Christmas in Wales*

Dylan Thomas

Years and years and years ago, when I was a boy, when there were wolves in Wales, and birds the color of red-flannel petticoats whisked past the harp-shaped hills, when we sang and wallowed all night and day in caves that smelt like Sunday afternoons in damp front farmhouse parlors, and we chased, with the jawbones of deacons, the English and the bears, before the motor car, before the wheel, before the duchess-faced horse, when we rode the daft and happy hills bareback, it snowed and it snowed. But here a small boy says: "It snowed last year, too. I made a snowman and my brother knocked it down and I knocked my brother down and then we had tea."

"But that was not the same snow," I say. "Our snow was not only shaken from whitewash buckets down the sky, it came shawling out of the ground and swam and drifted out of the arms and hands and bodies of the trees; snow grew overnight on the roofs of the houses like a pure and grandfather moss, minutely white-ivied the walls and settled on the postman, opening the gate, like a dumb, numb thunderstorm of white, torn Christmas cards."

"Were there postmen then, too?"

"With sprinkling eyes and wind-cherried noses, on spread, frozen feet they crunched up to the doors and mittened on them manfully. But all that the children could hear was a ringing of bells."

"You mean that the postman went rat-a-tat-tat and the doors rang?"

"I mean that the bells that the children could hear were inside them."

"I only hear thunder sometimes, never bells."

"There were church bells, too."

"Inside them?"

"No, no, no, in the bat-black, snow-white belfries, tugged by bishops and storks. And they rang their tidings over the bandaged town, over the frozen foam of the powder and ice-cream hills, over the crackling sea. It seemed that all the churches boomed for joy under my window; and the weather-cocks crew for Christmas, on our fence."

"Get back to the postmen."

"They were just ordinary postmen, fond of walking and dogs and Christmas and the snow. They knocked on the doors with blue knuckles. . . ."

"Ours has got a black knocker. . . ."

"And then they stood on the white Welcome mat in the little, drifted porches and huffed and puffed, making ghosts with their breath, and jogged from foot to foot like small boys wanting to go out."

"And then the Presents?"

"And then the Presents, after the Christmas box. And the cold postman, with a rose on his button-nose, tingled down the tea-tray slithered run of the chilly glinting hill. He went in his ice-bound boots like a man on fishmonger's slabs.

"He wagged his bag like a frozen camel's hump, dizzily turned the corner on one foot, and, by God, he was gone."

"Get back to the Presents."

"There were the Useful Presents: engulfing mufflers of the old coach days, and mittens made for giant sloths; zebra scarfs of a substance like silky gum that could be tug-o'-warred down to the galoshes; blinding tam-o'-shanters like patchwork tea cozies and bunny-suited busbies and bal-aclavas for victims of head-shrinking tribes; from aunts who always wore wool next to the skin there were mustached and rasping vests that made you wonder why the aunts had any skin left at all; and once I had a little crocheted nose bag from an aunt now, alas, no longer whinnying with us. And pictureless books in which small boys, though warned with quota-tions not to, *would* skate on Farmer Giles' pond and did and drowned; and books that told me everything about the wasp, except why."

"Go on to the Useless Presents."

"Bags of moist and many-colored jelly babies and a folded flag and a false nose and a tram-conductor's cap and a machine that punched tickets and rang a bell; never a catapult; once, by mistake that no one could explain, a little hatchet; and a celluloid duck that made, when you pressed it, a most unducklike sound, a mewing moo that an ambitious cat might make who wished to be a cow; and a painting book in which I could make the grass, the trees, the sea, and the animals any color I pleased, and still the dazzling sky-blue sheep are grazing in the red field under the rainbow-billed and pea-green birds. Hardboileds, toffee, fudge and allsorts, crunches, cracknels, humbugs, glaciers, marzipan, and butterwelsh for the Welsh. And troops of bright tin soldiers who, if they could not fight, could always run. And Snakes-and-Families and Happy Ladders. And Easy Hobbi-Games for Little Engineers, complete with instructions. Oh, easy for Leonardo!

"And a whistle to make the dogs bark to wake up the old man next door to make him beat on the wall with his stick to shake our picture off the wall. And a packet of cigarettes: you put one in your mouth and you stood at the corner of the street and you waited for hours, in vain, for an old lady to scold you for smoking a cigarette, and then with a smirk you ate it. And then it was breakfast under the balloons."

from *A Christmas Memory*

Truman Capote

Morning. Frozen rime lusters the grass; the sun, round as an orange and orange as hot-weather moons, balances on the horizon, burnishes the silvered winter woods. A wild turkey calls. A renegade hog grunts in the undergrowth. Soon, by the edge of the knee-deep, rapid-running water, we have to abandon the buggy. Queenie wades the stream first, paddles across barking complaints at the swiftness of the current, the pneumonia-making coldness of it. We follow, holding our shoes and equipment (a hatchet, a burlap sack) above our heads. A mile more: of chastising thorns, burs and briers that catch at our clothes; of rusty pine needles brilliant with gaudy fungus and molted feathers. Here, there, a flash, a flutter, an ecstasy of shrillings remind us that not all the birds have flown south. Always the path unwinds through lemony sun pools and pitch-black vine tunnels. Another creek to cross: a disturbed armada of speckled trout froths the water round us, and frogs the size of plates practice belly flops; beaver workmen are building a dam. On the farther shore, Queenie shakes herself and trembles. My friend shivers, too: not with cold but enthusiasm. One of her hat's ragged roses sheds a petal as she lifts her head and inhales the pine-heavy air. "We're almost there; can you smell it, Buddy?" she says, as though we were approaching an ocean.

And, indeed, it is a kind of ocean. Scented acres of holiday trees, prickly-leafed holly. Red berries shiny as Chinese bells: black crows swoop upon them screaming. Having stuffed our burlap sacks with enough greenery and crimson to garland a dozen windows, we set about choosing a tree. "It should be," muses my friend, "twice as tall as a boy. So a boy can't steal the

star." The one we pick is twice as tall as me. A brave handsome brute that survives thirty hatchet strokes before it keels with a creaking rending cry. Lugging it like a kill, we commence the long trek out. Every few yards we abandon the struggle, sit down and pant. But we have the strength of triumphant huntsmen; that and the tree's virile, icy perfume revive us, goad us on. Many complaints accompany our sunset return along the red clay road to town; but my friend is sly and noncommittal when passers-by praise the treasure perched in our buggy: what a fine tree and where did it come from? "Yonderways," she murmurs vaguely. Once a car stops and the rich mill owner's lazy wife leans out and whines: "Giveya two-bits cash for that ol tree." Ordinarily my friend is afraid of saying no; but on this occasion she promptly shakes her head: "We wouldn't take a dollar." The mill owner's wife persists. "A dollar, my foot! Fifty cents. That's my last offer. Goodness, woman, you can get another one." In answer, my friend gently reflects: "I doubt it. There's never two of anything."

We Wish You a Merry Christmas

Joyfully

1. We wish you a mer-ry Christ-mas, We wish you a mer-ry Christ-mas, We
2. Please bring us some fig-gy pud-ding, Please bring us some fig-gy pud-ding, Please
3. We won't go un-til we get some, We won't go un-til we get some, We

wish you a mer-ry Christ-mas, And a hap-py New Year!
bring us some fig-gy pud-ding, And bring it right here!
won't go un-til we get some, Please bring it right here!

"Dulce Domum"
from *The Wind in the Willows*

Kenneth Grahame

Mole's face beamed at the sight of all these objects so dear to him, and he hurried Rat through the door, lit a lamp in the hall, and took one glance round his old home. He saw the dust lying thick on everything, saw the cheerless, deserted look of the long-neglected house, and its narrow meagre dimensions, its worn and shabby contents—and collapsed again on a hall chair, his nose in his paws. "O, Ratty!" he cried dismally, "why ever did I do it? Why did I bring you to this poor, cold little place, on a night like this, when you might have been at River Bank by this time, toasting your toes before a blazing fire, with all your own nice things about you!"

The Rat paid no heed to his doleful self-reproaches. He was running here and there, opening doors, inspecting rooms and cupboards, and lighting lamps and candles and sticking them up everywhere. "What a capital little house this is!" he called out cheerily. "So compact! So well planned! Everything here and everything in its place! We'll make a jolly night of it. The first thing we want is a good fire; I'll see to that—I always know where to find things. So this is the parlour? Splendid! Your own idea, those little sleeping bunks in the wall? Capital! Now, I'll fetch the wood and the coals, and you get a duster, Mole—you'll find one in the drawer of the kitchen table—and try and smarten things up a bit. Bustle about, old chap!"

Encouraged by his inspiriting companion, the Mole roused himself and dusted and polished with energy and heartiness, while the Rat, running to and fro with armfuls of fuel, soon had a cheerful blaze roaring up the chimney. He hailed the Mole to come and warm himself; but Mole promptly had another fit of the blues, dropping down on a couch in dark despair and burying his face in his duster.

"Rat," he moaned, "how about your supper, you poor, cold, hungry, weary animal? I've nothing to give you—nothing—not a crumb!"

"What a fellow you are for giving in!" said the Rat reproachfully. "Why, only just now I saw a sardine opener on the kitchen dresser, quite distinctly; and everybody knows that means there are sardines about somewhere in the neighbourhood. Rouse yourself! pull yourself together, and come with me and forage."

They went and foraged accordingly, hunting through every cupboard and turning out every drawer. The result was not so very depressing after all, though of course it might have been better; a tin of sardines—a box of captain's biscuits, nearly full—and a German sausage encased in silver paper.

"There's a banquet for you!" observed the Rat, as he arranged the table. "I know some animals who would give their ears to be sitting down to supper with us tonight!"

"No bread!" groaned the Mole dolorously; "no butter, no—"

"No *pâte de foie gras*, no champagne!" continued the Rat, grinning. "And that reminds me—what's the little door at the end of the passage? Your cellar, of course! Every luxury in this house! Just you wait a minute."

He made for the cellar door, and presently reappeared, somewhat dusty, with a bottle of beer in each paw and another under each arm. "Self-indulgent beggar you seem to be, Mole," he observed. "Deny yourself nothing. This is really the jolliest little place I ever was in. Now, wherever did you pick up those prints? Make the place look so home-like, they do. No wonder you're so fond of it, Mole. Tell us all about it, and how you came to make it what it is."

Then, while the Rat busied himself fetching plates, and knives and forks, and mustard which he mixed in an egg-cup, the Mole, his bosom still heaving with the stress of his recent emotion, related—somewhat shyly at first, but with more freedom as he warmed to his subject—how this was planned, and how that was thought out, and how this was got through a windfall from an aunt, and that was a wonderful find and a bargain, and this other thing was bought out of laborious savings and a certain amount of "going without." His spirits finally quite restored, he must needs go and caress his possessions, and take a lamp and show off their points to his visitor and expatiate on them, quite forgetful of the supper they both so much needed; Rat who was desperately hungry but strove to conceal it, nodding seriously, examining with a puckered brow, and saying, "Wonderful," and "Most remarkable," at intervals, when the chance for an observation was given him.

At last the Rat succeeded in decoying him to the table, and had just got seriously to work with the sardine opener when sounds were heard from the forecourt without—sounds like the scuffling of small feet in the gravel and a confused murmur of tiny voices, while broken sentences reached them—"Now, all in a line—hold the lantern up a bit, Tommy—clear your throats first—no coughing after I say one, two, three.—Where's young Bill?—Here, come on, do, we're all a-waiting—"

"What's up?" inquired the Rat, pausing in his labours.

"I think it must be the field mice," replied the Mole, with a touch of pride in his manner. "They go round carol singing regularly at this time of the year. They're quite an institution in these parts. And they never pass me over—they come to Mole End last of all; and I used to give them hot drinks, and supper too sometimes, when I could afford it. It will be like old times to hear them again."

"Let's have a look at them!" cried the Rat, jumping up and running to the door.

It was a pretty sight, and a seasonable one, that met their eyes when they flung the door open. In the forecourt, lit by the dim rays of a horn lantern, some eight or ten little field mice stood in a semicircle, red worsted comforters round their throats, their forepaws thrust deep into their pockets, their feet jigging for warmth. With bright beady eyes they glanced shyly at each other, sniggering a little, sniffing and applying coat sleeves a good deal. As the door opened, one of the elder ones that carried the lantern was just saying, "Now then, one, two, three!" and forthwith their shrill little voices uprose on the air, singing one of the old-time carols that their forefathers composed in fields that were fallow and held by frost, or when snowbound in chimney corners, and handed down to be sung in the miry street to lamplit windows at Yuletime.

Carol

Villagers all, this frosty tide,
Let your doors swing open wide,
Though wind may follow, and snow beside,
Yet draw us in by your fire to bide;
   Joy shall be yours in the morning!

Here we stand in the cold and the sleet,
Blowing fingers and stamping feet,
Come from far away you to greet—
You by the fire and we in the street—
   Bidding you joy in the morning!

For ere one half of the night was gone,
Sudden a star has led us on,
Raining bliss and benison—
Bliss tomorrow and more anon,
   Joy for every morning!

Goodman Joseph toiled through the snow—
Saw the star o'er a stable low;
Mary she might not further go—
Welcome thatch and litter below!
   Joy was hers in the morning!

And then they heard the angels tell
"Who were the first to cry Nowell?
Animals all, as it befell,
In the stable where they did dwell!
    Joy shall be theirs in the morning!"

The voices ceased, the singers, bashful but smiling, exchanged sidelong glances, and silence succeeded—but for a moment only. Then, from up above and far away, down the tunnel they had so lately travelled was borne to their ears in a faint musical hum the sound of distant bells ringing a joyful and clangorous peal.

"Very well sung, boys!" cried the Rat heartily. "And now come along in, all of you, and warm yourselves by the fire, and have something hot!"

"Yes, come along, field mice," cried the Mole eagerly. "This is quite like old times! Shut the door after you. Pull up that settle to the fire. Now, you just wait a minute, while we—O, Ratty!" he cried in despair, plumping down on a seat, with tears impending. "Whatever are we doing? We've nothing to give them!"

"You leave all that to me," said the masterful Rat. "Here, you with the lantern! Come over this way. I want to talk to you. Now, tell me, are there any shops open at this hour of the night?"

"Why, certainly, sir," replied the field mouse respectfully. "At this time of the year our shops keep open to all sorts of hours."

"Then look here!" said the Rat. "You go off at once, you and your lantern, and you get me—"

Here much muttered conversation ensued, and the Mole only heard bits of it, such as—"Fresh, mind!—no, a pound of that will do—see you get Buggins's, for I won't have any other—no, only the best—if you can't get it there, try somewhere else—yes, of course, home-made, no tinned stuff—well then do the best you can!" Finally, there was a chink of coins passing from paw to paw, the field mouse was provided with an ample basket for his purchases, and off he hurried, he and his lantern.

The rest of the field mice, perched in a row on the settle, their small legs swinging, gave themselves up to enjoyment of the fire, and toasted their chilblains till they tingled; while the Mole, failing to draw them into easy conversation, plunged into family history and made each of them recite the names of his numerous brothers who were too young, it appeared, to be allowed to go out a-carolling this year, but looked forward very shortly to winning the parental consent.

The Rat, meanwhile, was busy examining the label on one of the beer bottles. "I perceive this to be Old Burton," he remarked approvingly. "*Sensible* Mole! The very thing! Now we shall be able to mull some ale! Get the things ready, Mole, while I draw the corks."

It did not take long to prepare the brew and thrust the tin heater well into the red heart of the fire; and soon every field mouse was sipping and coughing and choking (for a little mulled ale goes a long way) and wiping his eyes and laughing and forgetting he had ever been cold in all his life.

"They act plays too, these fellows," the Mole explained to the Rat. "Make them up all by themselves, and act them afterward. And very well they do it, too! They gave us a capital one last year, about a field mouse who was captured at sea by a Barbary corsair, and made to row in a galley; and when he escaped and got home again, his ladylove had gone into a convent. Here, *you!* You were in it, I remember. Get up and recite a bit."

The field mouse addressed got up on his legs, giggled shyly, looked round the room, and remained absolutely tongue-tied. His comrades cheered him on, Mole coaxed and encouraged him, and the Rat went so far as to take him by the shoulders and shake him; but nothing could overcome his stage fright. They were all busily engaged on him like watermen applying the Royal Humane Society's regulation to a case of long submersion, when the latch clicked, the door opened, and the field mouse with the lantern reappeared, staggering under the weight of his basket.

There was no more talk of play-acting once the very real and solid contents of the basket had been tumbled out on the table. Under the generalship of Rat, everybody was set to do something or to fetch something. In a very few minutes supper was ready, and Mole, as he took the head of the table in a sort of dream, saw a lately barren board set thick with savoury comforts; saw his little friends' faces brighten and beam as they fell to without delay; and then let himself loose—for he was famished indeed—on the provender so magically provided, thinking what a happy homecoming this had turned out, after all. As they ate, they talked of old times, and the field mice gave him the local gossip up to date, and answered as well as they could the hundred questions he had to ask them. The Rat said little or nothing, only taking care that each guest had what he wanted, and plenty of it, and that Mole had no trouble or anxiety about anything.

They clattered off at last, very grateful and showering wishes of the season, with their jacket pockets stuffed with remembrances for the small brothers and sisters at home. When the door had closed on the last of them and the chink of the lanterns had died away, Mole and Rat kicked the fire up, drew their chairs in, brewed themselves a last nightcap of mulled ale, and discussed the events of the long day. At last the Rat, with a tremendous yawn, said, "Mole, old chap, I'm ready to drop. Sleepy is simply not the word. That your own bunk over on that side? Very well, then, I'll take this.

What a ripping little house this is! Everything so handy!"

He clambered into his bunk and rolled himself well up in the blankets, and slumber gathered him forthwith, as a swath of barley is folded into the arms of the reaping machine.

The weary Mole also was glad to turn in without delay, and soon had his head on his pillow, in great joy and contentment. But ere he closed his eyes he let them wander round his old room, mellow in the glow of the firelight that played or rested on familiar and friendly things which had long been unconsciously a part of him, and now smilingly received him back, without rancour. He was now in just the frame of mind that the tactful Rat had quietly worked to bring about in him. He saw clearly how plain and simple—how narrow, even—it all was; but clearly, too, how much it all meant to him, and the special value of some such anchorage in one's existence. He did not at all want to abandon the new life and its splendid spaces, to turn his back on sun and air and all they offered him and creep home and stay there; the upper world was all too strong, it called to him still, even down there, and he knew he must return to the larger stage. But it was good to think he had this to come back to, this place which was all his own, these things which were so glad to see him again and could always be counted upon for the same simple welcome.

from *A Christmas Carol*

Charles Dickens

Well! Never mind so long as you are come," said Mrs. Cratchit. "Sit ye down before the fire, my dear, and have a warm, Lord bless ye!"

"No, no! There's father coming," cried the two young Cratchits, who were everywhere at once. "Hide, Martha, hide!"

So Martha hid herself, and in came little Bob, the father, with at least three feet of comforter exclusive of the fringe, hanging down before him; and his threadbare clothes darned up and brushed, to look seasonable; and Tiny Tim upon his shoulder. Alas for Tiny Tim, he bore a little crutch, and had his limbs supported by an iron frame!

"Why, where's our Martha?" cried Bob Cratchit, looking round.

"Not coming," said Mrs. Cratchit.

"Not coming!" said Bob, with a sudden declension in his high spirits; for he had been Tim's blood horse all the way from church, and had come home rampant. "Not coming upon Christmas Day!"

Martha didn't like to see him disappointed, if it were only in joke; so she came out prematurely from behind the closet door, and ran into his arms, while the two young Cratchits hustled Tiny Tim, and bore him off into the wash-house, that he might hear the pudding singing in the copper.

"And how did little Tim behave?" asked Mrs. Cratchit, when she had rallied Bob on his credulity, and Bob had hugged his daughter to his heart's content.

"As good as gold," said Bob, "and better. Somehow he gets thoughtful, sitting by himself so much, and thinks the strangest things you ever heard. He told me, coming home, that he hoped the people saw him in the church, because he was a cripple, and it might be pleasant to them to remember upon Christmas Day, who made lame beggars walk, and blind men see."

Bob's voice was tremulous when he told them this, and trembled more when he said that Tiny Tim was growing strong and hearty.

His active little crutch was heard upon the floor, and back came Tiny Tim before another word was spoken, escorted by his brother and sister to his stool before the fire; and while Bob, turning up his cuffs—as if, poor fellow, they were capable of being made more shabby—compounded some hot mixture in a jug with gin and lemons, and stirred it round and round and put it on the hob to simmer; Master Peter, and the two ubiquitous young Cratchits went to fetch the goose, with which they soon returned in high procession.

Such a bustle ensued that you might have thought a goose the rarest of all birds; a feathered phenomenon, to which a black swan was a matter of course—and in truth it was something very like it in that house. Mrs. Cratchit made the gravy (ready beforehand in a little saucepan) hissing hot; Master Peter mashed the potatoes with incredible vigour; Miss Belinda sweetened up the apple-sauce; Martha dusted the hot plates; Bob took Tiny Tim beside him in a tiny corner at the table; the two young Cratchits set chairs for everybody, not forgetting themselves, and mounting guard upon their posts, crammed spoons into their mouths, lest they should shriek for goose before their turn came to be helped. At last the dishes were set on, and grace was said. It was succeeded by a breathless pause, as Mrs. Cratchit, looking slowly all along the carving-knife, prepared to plunge it in the breast; but when she did, and when the long expected gust of stuffing issued forth, one murmur of delight arose all round the board, and even Tiny Tim, excited by the two young Cratchits, beat on the table with the handle of his knife, and feebly cried Hurrah!

There never was such a goose. Bob said he didn't believe there ever was such a goose cooked. Its tenderness and flavour, size and cheapness, were the themes of universal admiration. Eked out by apple-sauce and mashed potatoes, it was a sufficient dinner for the whole family; indeed, as Mrs. Cratchit said with great delight (surveying one small atom of a bone upon the dish), they hadn't ate it all at last! Yet every one had had enough, and the youngest Cratchits in particular, were steeped in sage and onion to the eyebrows! But now, the plates being changed by Miss Belinda, Mrs. Cratchit left the room alone—too nervous to bear witnesses—to take the pudding up and bring it in.

Suppose it should not be done enough! Suppose it should break in turning out! Suppose somebody should have got over the wall of the back-

yard, and stolen it, while they were merry with the goose—a supposition at which the two young Cratchits became livid! All sorts of horrors were supposed.

Hallo! A great deal of steam! The pudding was out of the copper. A smell like a washing-day! That was the cloth. A smell like an eating-house and a pastrycook's next door to each other, with a laundress's next door to that! That was the pudding! In half a minute Mrs. Cratchit entered—flushed, but smiling proudly—with the pudding, like a speckled cannon-ball, so hard and firm, blazing in half of half-a-quartern of ignited brandy, and bedight with Christmas holly stuck into the top.

Oh, a wonderful pudding! Bob Cratchit said, and calmly too, that he regarded it as the greatest success achieved by Mrs. Cratchit since their marriage. Mrs. Cratchit said that now the weight was off her mind, she would confess she had had her doubts about the quantity of flour. Everybody had something to say about it, but nobody said or thought it was at all a small pudding for a large family. It would have been flat heresy to do so. Any Cratchit would have blushed to hint at such a thing.

At last the dinner was all done, the cloth was cleared, the hearth swept, and the fire made up. The compound in the jug being tasted, and considered perfect, apples and oranges were put upon the table, and a shovel-full of chestnuts on the fire. Then all the Cratchit family drew round the hearth, in what Bob Cratchit called a circle, meaning half a one; and at Bob Cratchit's elbow stood the family display of glass. Two tumblers, and a custard-cup without a handle.

These held the hot stuff from the jug, however, as well as golden goblets would have done; and Bob served it out with beaming looks, while the chestnuts on the fire sputtered and cracked noisily. Then Bob proposed:

"A Merry Christmas to us all, my dears. God bless us!"

Which all the family re-echoed.

"God bless us every one!" said Tiny Tim, the last of all.

The Twelve Days of Christmas

Traditional

The first day of Christmas
My true love sent to me
A partridge in a pear tree.

The second day of Christmas
My true love sent to me
Two turtle doves, and
A partridge in a pear tree.

The third day of Christmas
My true love sent to me
Three French hens,
Two turtle doves, and
A partridge in a pear tree.

The fourth day of Christmas
My true love sent to me
Four colly birds,
Three French hens,
Two turtle doves, and
A partridge in a pear tree.

The fifth day of Christmas
My true love sent to me
Five gold rings,
Four colly birds,
Three French hens,
Two turtle doves, and
A partridge in a pear tree.

The sixth day of Christmas
My true love sent to me
Six geese a-laying,
Five gold rings,
Four colly birds,
Three French hens,
Two turtle doves, and
A partridge in a pear tree.

The seventh day of Christmas
My true love sent to me
Seven swans a-swimming,
Six geese a-laying,
Five gold rings,
Four colly birds,
Three French hens,
Two turtle doves, and
A partridge in a pear tree.

The eighth day of Christmas
My true love sent to me
Eight maids a-milking,
Seven swans a-swimming,
Six geese a-laying,
Five gold rings,
Four colly birds,
Three French hens,
Two turtle doves, and
A partridge in a pear tree.

The ninth day of Christmas
My true love sent to me
Nine drummers drumming,
Eight maids a-milking,
Seven swans a-swimming,
Six geese a-laying,
Five gold rings,
Four colly birds,
Three French hens,
Two turtle doves, and
A partridge in a pear tree.

The tenth day of Christmas
My true love sent to me
Ten pipers piping,
Nine drummers drumming,
Eight maids a-milking,
Seven swans a-swimming,
Six geese a-laying,
Five gold rings,
Four colly birds,
Three French hens,
Two turtle doves, and
A partridge in a pear tree.

The eleventh day of Christmas
My true love sent to me
Eleven ladies dancing,
Ten pipers piping,
Nine drummers drumming,
Eight maids a-milking,
Seven swans a-swimming,
Six geese a-laying,
Five gold rings,
Four colly birds,
Three French hens,
Two turtle doves, and
A partridge in a pear tree.

The twelfth day of Christmas
My true love sent to me
Twelve lords a-leaping,
Eleven ladies dancing,
Ten pipers piping,
Nine drummers drumming,
Eight maids a-milking,
Seven swans a-swimming,
Six geese a-laying,
Five gold rings,
Four colly birds,
Three French hens,
Two turtle doves, and
A partridge in a pear tree.